Redeemed

A Journey *from* Brokenness to Freedom

ROSE METHENY

Redeemed: A Journey from Brokenness to Freedom
© 2025 Rose Metheny
All rights reserved.

Cover Design & Interior Layout: Brandi Lariscy-Avant
Published by: Grace and Glow Press

Scripture References:
Unless otherwise noted, all Scripture is taken from the New Living Translation (NLT) and the English Standard Version (ESV).

ISBN 979-8-9992180-0-1

This book is a work of nonfiction, born from one sacred morning of journaling during prayer. It reflects the author's real-life experiences, personal memories, and intimate faith journey. Some names and identifying details have been changed to protect the privacy of those involved.

For speaking inquiries, bulk orders, or to connect with Rose:
www.rosemetheny.com | hello@rosemetheny.com

DEDICATION

To the One who found me in the dark,
held me through the pain,
and called me by name—
Jesus, my Redeemer.
This is all for You.
Every word. Every tear. Every victory.
Thank You for never giving up on me.

To my husband, Larry —
my rock, my hero, my protector.
Your steady love, quiet strength, and unwavering support have carried
me through more than words can say.

Thank you for standing beside me through the storms,
for covering me in prayer,
and for loving me like Jesus does.
You are a gift I'll never stop thanking God for.

To my beautiful mama—
your love has been a shelter, your prayers a lifeline, and your faith an
anchor for my heart.
Thank you for every prayer you whispered over me, every tear you
cried for me. I love you more than words could ever say, and I
thank God every day for the gift of being your daughter.

To every soul who's ever believed the lie that you're too broken, too
far gone, or too unworthy to be loved—
may these pages lead you into the arms of the One who has never
stopped loving you.
He sees you. He knows you. He heals. And He sets you free.

TABLE OF CONTENTS

One—The Silence That Shaped Me *1*

In this chapter, you'll step into the quiet world of a little girl who lived in fear—too afraid to speak, too ashamed to be seen. Trauma silenced her, and the silence followed her everywhere. If you've ever felt like your pain was ignored or your voice didn't matter, this chapter will speak straight to your heart.

Two—The Girl No One Protected *8*

This is the story of a child who was not only hurt—but left unprotected by the very people who should have fought for her. Abuse, betrayal, and abandonment became familiar. If you've ever felt invisible or abandoned, you'll find yourself in these pages—and begin to see how God never left.

Three—Trying to Feel Alive *9*

In the aftermath of pain, she chased anything that made her feel something—addiction, chaos, and relationships that only deepened the wound. This chapter exposes the lie that the world's comfort can heal what only Jesus can reach. If you've ever tried to outrun your pain, you'll know this story well.

This final chapter is a declaration—a song of freedom. Not because life became perfect, but because Christ made her whole. You'll be reminded that freedom isn't a feeling—it's a promise. And it's yours too. Because Jesus still meets people at the well. And He's waiting for you.

*This is a raw, unedited glimpse into the darkest place I've ever been— written before healing, before hope, before I knew Jesus. **It's not polished. It's not pretty. (Please be advised)**. It's the truth as I lived it. I share it because someone needs to know even in the middle of the pain, when it feels like freedom is impossible… Jesus still comes. And He still redeems.*

THE WOMAN AT THE WELL

(John 4:1–42)

"Whoever drinks of the water that I shall give him will never thirst. But the water that I shall give him will become in him a fountain of water springing up into everlasting life." —John 4:14

Before you step into these pages, I want to take you to a well in Samaria.

There, in the heat of the day, a weary and broken woman came to draw water. But instead of avoiding shame, she encountered Jesus. He asked her for a drink, then offered her living water—a gift that would never run dry.

He revealed the truth of her past, yet offered her hope, not condemnation. He showed her that worship was no longer about places or traditions, but about spirit and truth. Then He spoke words that would change her life forever: "I who speak to you am He."

She left her water jar behind and ran to tell others: "Come, see a man who told me everything I ever did. Could this be the Christ?" Many believed because of her testimony. Others came to hear for themselves and declared: "This is indeed the Christ, the Savior of the world."

This is where redemption begins—with Jesus, who meets us in our brokenness, offers us living water, and turns our story into a testimony.

PROLOGUE

Before Jesus

Before I met Jesus, I didn't want to live.

I wasn't just lost—I was completely broken. My life was constant chaos. Everything hurt. My mind was a room full of screaming monkeys. I couldn't sleep. I couldn't think. I couldn't catch a breath without feeling like I was drowning.

I tried everything to shut it down—drugs, casual relationships, distractions, more drugs. One night, I overdosed. I shouldn't have survived, but somehow I did. To this day, I believe it was the hand of God on me.

I had multiple abortions and carried a shame so deep.

I hated myself. I hated my life. I felt unworthy, used, and invisible. And deep down, I believed I was unlovable.

I truly didn't think I'd ever be okay.

But then—Jesus.

He didn't wait for me to get it together. He didn't ask me to clean myself up first. He came right into the middle of my mess—into the wreckage, the shame, the numbness. And He didn't flinch.

He didn't shame me. He didn't turn away. He loved me when I didn't know how to be loved.

And slowly, He began to heal me—piece by piece.

The screaming in my head started to quiet. The shame began to lift. And the regret that had weighed me down for so long began to lose its grip.

I'm not the same person I used to be. I'm not perfect—but I'm free. And *that's* what redemption looks like.

This book is my story—messy, painful, real. But it's also a story of what God can do when you let Him in.

If you've ever felt too far gone, too broken, or too ashamed—this is for you. Jesus changed everything for me. And He can do the same for you.

> *"He reached down from heaven and rescued me; he drew me out of deep waters."* —Psalm 18:16

> *"He heals the brokenhearted and binds up their wounds."* —Psalm 147:3

> *"I will restore to you the years that the swarming locust has eaten."* —Joel 2:25

> *"Therefore, if anyone is in Christ, he is a new creation; the old has passed away, and behold, the new has come."* —2 Corinthians 5:17

Introduction

I never set out to write a book.

Honestly, I didn't even think I had a voice—let alone a story worth telling.

But one morning, during prayer and devotion, the words just poured out.

It started as a journal entry—raw, honest, and deeply personal.

I was simply pouring my heart out to Jesus.

And that morning's journaling became *Redeemed*.

This isn't a memoir.

It's not a perfectly polished timeline of my life.

It's a moment. A holy moment where God met me in the middle of my brokenness and gently began to write a new story with my pain.

If you've ever felt like you're too far gone…

If you've ever carried shame so heavy it silenced your soul…

If you've ever wondered whether healing is possible for someone like you—this is for you.

Redeemed isn't a formula or a fix.

It's a glimpse into what happens when we let God into the places we've tried to hide.

It's a sacred, sometimes messy, always holy journey from brokenness to freedom.

At the end of the chapters, you'll find a Pause & Reflect section—with scripture, prayer, and journal prompts to help you walk through your own healing.

Take your time. Don't rush. Let Jesus meet you there.

I don't know your whole story… but I do know this:

You are not too broken. You are not too far gone.

And you are absolutely not beyond redemption.

Jesus came for people just like us—

The tired. The ashamed. The broken. The ones who wonder if they'll ever feel whole.

This is my story.

But it's also your invitation.

To trade shame for grace.

To trade silence for truth.

To trade bondage for freedom.

To be redeemed.

With all my heart,
Rose

Author's Note

What you're about to read is the original journal entry I wrote on November 6, 2006—the morning God met me in the middle of my brokenness. I didn't know then that this raw outpouring would one day become the heartbeat of a book. But I knew He was doing something. This was the morning I first dared to believe I could be truly, fully redeemed.

At that time, I had already given my life to Jesus. I was walking with Him, praying daily, and clinging to His Word. But that morning hit different. I wasn't writing from a place of new belief —I was writing as a Christian woman still carrying wounds that hadn't healed, still wrestling with shame I didn't know how to release. It was during that sacred time of prayer and devotion that the floodgates opened - and what poured out was honest, unfiltered, and Spirit-led.

This wasn't a story I planned to tell. It wasn't meant to be a book. It was simply my heart, laid bare before the Lord. A cry for freedom. A surrender I didn't even know I was ready for. And somehow, in His mercy, He turned that cry into a testimony.

As I turned this journal into a book, I added chapter breaks to help guide the reader through the story. But originally, there were no chapters—just one sacred, uninterrupted outpouring of my heart.

The Silence That Shaped Me

This morning, during prayer and devotion, I cried out to the Lord: "Lord, what do you want from me?" And His answer came so clearly: "Freedom."

I had been reading about failure and redemption—exactly what my weary heart needed to hear.

When I think about failure, my mind floods with memories of choices I regret. Things I wish I could undo. The years caught up in addiction—drugs became my escape, but nearly destroyed me. I wasn't the mother my son deserved—I was too high, too broken, too lost in shame to be present the way he needed. I distanced myself from my family, not because I didn't love them, but because I couldn't bear to face them carrying so much guilt, pain, and emptiness. I had multiple abortions—each one carving deeper wounds I didn't know how to grieve. I stayed with men who hit me, used me, broke me—thinking that was all I was worth. My life was a cycle of chaos and regret. The illusion of escape. The downward spiral I once danced with, believing it would never stop. The self-destructive patterns. The way I've mistreated myself—and allowed others to do the same. The inner critic, the deep sadness, the impossible expectations I placed on myself. The haunting question: "Why can't I just be someone else?"

But something was different today. In the quiet of that sacred moment, I felt the Lord gently prompting me: It's time to face this.

And just like before, I wanted to run. To shove it back down. To pretend it never happened. I had spent years trying to outrun the truth—numbing, hiding, dissociating—doing anything but looking in the mirror.

But God, in His mercy, wasn't asking me to relive the pain. He was inviting me to release it.

It's strange how the things we try so hard to forget are the things that seem to never leave us.

I've spent so much of my life pretending certain things didn't happen. I was so young. So afraid. The fear from those early years is hard to explain. It's a feeling that doesn't easily fade.

I wanted to forget. But I've found it hard to truly live or breathe freely with that kind of weight always lingering.

The memories. The fear. The shame. They've stayed with me—woven into the background of my every decision.

For a long time, I believed that if I didn't think about it, it couldn't hurt me. If I didn't speak it out loud, maybe it wouldn't define me.

But I went through things as a little girl that no child should ever go through. Terrifying things. And it wasn't a stranger—it was someone who was supposed to protect me.

It left me confused, scared, and shut down. It twisted my view of love, trust, safety—everything.

And it didn't stop when I got older. The pain just changed shape. It followed me. Got heavier. Got darker.

I never talked about it. Not even in a whisper. But no matter how much I've tried to lock it away, it followed me.

It was there in my decisions. In my relationships. In the way I saw myself. In the way I thought. In how I navigated the world.

I got older, but inside I was still that terrified little girl that no one protected. Eventually, I shut down completely. Numb. Detached. Gone—but still breathing.

There are entire pieces of my childhood I don't remember. Some memories return in fragments. It's something called dissociation—a way the mind protects itself.

And honestly… there were times I wished I could stay in that numb space forever. Because feeling meant facing. And facing meant falling apart.

Suicidal thoughts hovered over me since childhood. I'm deeply grateful now that I never had the courage to act on them. But the struggle? It's been with me for as long as I can remember.

Growing up without my dad left a bigger mark than I once believed. I used to think it didn't matter. But now, as an adult—and a mom—I see just how much it did.

I remember how much I wanted to be around him. My family says I'd sit at the window waiting for him to come. I don't remember that. I don't remember him not showing up.

My weekends with him were always the same—meeting new women and trying to remember their names. There was always someone new. He had no boundaries. He'd talk to me about things no child should hear. The kind of conversations that made me want to disappear into the carpet.

I never liked that.

The picture on the bathroom wall wouldn't leave my mind this morning, either. It was a pastel drawing of a wooden lounge chair on the beach. Pastel blue sky. Pastel pink umbrella. The ocean looked like it went on forever.

We were at a family party. My abuser took me to the bathroom. I wasn't safe—even in a house full of people. I was 8.

Then came the memory of the video store we once owned. The liquor store owner two doors down had always made me uncomfortable. He'd tell me I was "so beautiful" every time I went in. I hated it. I never looked him in the eyes.

One afternoon, I walked in to buy candy—something I'd done a hundred times before. As I handed him money, he grabbed my arm and pulled it down hard. Pain shot through it—I thought he'd broken it. He tried to pull me toward the back room, his grip tight on my arms and waist.

But that day... Something inside me snapped. I fought. I remember fighting for the first time—and getting away. I ran next door in tears and told my mom and stepdad what happened.

But they didn't react. They just told me not to go there again. No police report. No confrontation. Just silence.

I remember my mom looking so scared... so helpless. She didn't know how to protect me. And I didn't know how to ask her to.

When I was in the ninth grade, my school counselor advised my family to attend family therapy. I spent more time in the counselor's office than I did in class when I went to class.

I remember that lady. I frustrated her because I never said anything. She talked. And talked. I listened—maybe. But I never said a word. I would just sit there, arms folded, eyes down. I didn't have the language for my pain. Just a locked heart and a silent scream.

Eventually, she referred us to what was supposed to be family therapy, I think? But my family never went in—just me.

And what followed with this new guy seemed to be part of the script.

He was in his 50s or 60s. Looked like Santa Claus—white beard, white hair, round. I hated Santa Claus. I still do.

I remember sitting in his office, completely shut down, while he said things no child should ever hear. He told me that he "would love to make love to me." Said I "deserved to be loved."

That's all he said. Or maybe that's all I heard. My mind left the room. My body stayed. I just sat there, staring at my hands. Numb. Trapped.

They kept taking me to see him for a few months. Then we just stopped going.

Another adult who should've helped—but didn't. Another betrayal added to the pile.

Then I started thinking about when I was 14... and that older man. A family friend. He was 29. Funny how I remember his age—but not his name.

I wanted a cigarette. He offered one and said he'd drive me to get it.

He took me to a garage—some random place he said was connected to his ex-girlfriend's father, someone who had recently passed away under tragic circumstances.

I didn't want to go in. I felt uneasy the moment we got there. But I stayed quiet.

He kept talking. Tried to make it seem normal. But nothing about it was.

And once we were inside... something happened that broke something deeper in me. I didn't scream. I didn't run. I just shut down—again.

I remember the look on his face afterward. Like nothing had happened. Like we were just picking up where we left off in the conversation.

And I sat there, frozen. It felt like another piece of me died that day. Like I disappeared—but my body stayed behind.

Then there was another day...

My boyfriend at the time forced himself on me. We were in a room where my stepsisters were—pretending not to hear or see anything.

I remember crying. Begging him to stop. But he didn't.

What I remember most isn't even what he did. It was the fact that they let it happen.

They laughed. They heard me. They knew.

But I wasn't crying because of him—I was crying because no one protected me.

No one stepped in. No one said, "That's not okay." No one stood up for me.

And when it was over… I shut down again. Completely quiet. Like always. Another silence added to a long line of silences.

Sometimes I wonder what they remember about that day. If they remember anything at all.

But I do.

After that, something in me shifted. My heart didn't feel the same. I didn't feel the same.

I remember crying a lot at first—Tears on the outside. Silent sobs in the dark.

But over time, the tears stopped. And I only cried inside.

I think part of me died when the abuse first started—maybe as early as 4 years old. Maybe that's why I never fought back. Why I didn't speak up. Why I didn't scream when others hurt me later.

I wasn't a fighter. I wish I had been.

Maybe I could've protected myself. Maybe I could've run.

But somewhere along the way…I lost my voice.

I don't know exactly when. But I know that somewhere in the silence, in the shame, in the survival…

I stopped believing I was worth saving.

Two

The Girl No One Protected

Then my thoughts turned to my grandfather. He was a harsh, angry man. His words to me were like a broken record. He yelled every single day—from the time I was ten until the day I left at eighteen. With a baby. He would even slap me when I dared to question him.

And my mom? She couldn't make him stop. She was still afraid of him—even as a grown woman, even in her own home. She had lived with that fear her entire life. So to her, it was just normal. Just the way things were. Good or bad. Right or wrong.

But I always wondered…Why didn't anyone stand up for me? Why didn't anyone protect me?

Eventually, I stopped wondering. Eventually, I just assumed it was because I wasn't worth protecting.

Three

Trying to Feel Alive

Over the years, I stayed silent. I believed that if you didn't speak about it, it was like it never happened. Saying it out loud would make it real. Too painful.

And oh, the choices I made after…

The drug addiction. The toxic relationships. The spiral of self-destruction.

The story just kept repeating itself. I was still that same shut-down, scared little girl—just trying to be a woman.

And the truth is…I hated myself. I didn't want to live.

Four

I Lost Myself

But in many ways, I already felt like I was gone.

"What do You want from me, Lord?" I asked.

And He answered—clearly. Not a whisper this time. But a firm, loving word:

"Freedom."

Five

The Woman at the Well

I think often about the Samaritan woman at the well. How afraid she must've been. The Bible says she went there alone—after the other women had already come and gone. She didn't want to face the gossip. The judgment. The stares.

She chose to go when no one else would be there.

I imagine her heart was heavy. Full of shame. Tired of being the one no one would stand up for.

I know that feeling. The feeling of having no voice. Of knowing no one would defend you. Of living in fear that no one would care enough to protect you.

It's easy to pick on someone who never says a word. Who stays quiet. Who feels invisible.

But Jesus saw her. And He saw me.

It doesn't matter how many times I've read her story…How many times I've studied this passage…Every single time, my heart connects with hers.

I can feel her trying to steady her breath, doing everything she could to hold back the tears. And when she couldn't anymore—I can feel the sting of those tears as they fell.

In the Gospel of John, we're told she had five husbands. And the man she was living with when she met Jesus wasn't her husband.

I know this woman. Honestly, if I could be transported back to Bible times, I probably would've been her.

I know what it's like to carry pain and shame. To try and hide it. To crave love. To just want to feel normal.

Oh, I can feel the fire in her soul. **Five husbands.**

Maybe she tried to love husband #1, but he didn't love her. Maybe being with him broke her more and more. And maybe that's what led her to husband #2. In her attempt to find love and be loved, maybe her broken spirit gave in to the first one who promised it. Maybe her first love lived in husband #2… but perhaps he betrayed it.

By the time she found husband #3, she was probably so shut down, so clingy, needy, and desperate that he couldn't take it. Or maybe he was abusive. Either way, she was rejected again.

Then came husband #4—maybe he knew her story and just saw an opportunity. No love, no commitment…just someone to bed. By this point, I can see her heart: broken, used, abused, tired. All she wanted was love. Someone to choose her. To accept her.

She ran from relationship to relationship hoping to find love. Longing to be whole. Longing to feel anything.

And then there was husband #5. Did he love her? I don't know. But neither did she. She couldn't. How could she? She didn't even love herself.

In fact… I'm almost sure she hated herself.

So maybe husband #5 didn't even matter. Any hope for real love was long gone. She just needed security. Somewhere to rest her head at night.

But when you don't love yourself, you don't know how to love. Maybe she was clingy and desperate. Or maybe she was tired, hard, and sarcastic.

I don't know. But I do know this: She was afraid. Full of shame. And the man she was with when she met Jesus… was not her husband.

So on that one day when she arrived later than the others to draw water, she walked straight into the arms of Love itself but didn't even know it.

I can see her eyes meeting His. Eyes that didn't look down on her. Eyes that didn't want anything from her.

And in that moment… I believe she knew. She didn't know what it meant yet. But she knew something was different.

I can almost see her face when Jesus began to speak…When He told her what He knew.

Not just her past. But her heart. Everything her empty eyes had been revealing all along.

Six

When He Found Me

Before I knew Jesus, I couldn't look anyone in the eyes. Out of fear. Definitely out of shame.

But on that day, when the Samaritan woman looked into His eyes… I could feel her heart begin to melt. Melt away the hardness. Melt away the armor she wore to protect herself. Melt away the walls she had built around her heart.

It's true when Scripture says, **"Jesus Christ is the glory and the lifter of our heads."** Only in Him is there real, lasting freedom.

"Come to Me," He says, *"…you who labor and are heavy laden. Come."*

All that work we do…Trying to fix this. Trying to fix that. Manically attempting to control this, control that. Working here and there just to forget, to hide, to run.

Work, work, work!

And He says—**Come.**

What started as a simple conversation at the well turned into a divine appointment. Jesus got right to the root. And He offered her living water—Water that becomes a spring within, flowing with eternal life.

That moment revealed her true desire. All her life's longing. All her efforts. All her hope—They were answered in that water. **Living water that gives life.**

When I close my eyes, I see her running. Not away this time. This time… she was running to.

I can hear her breath—short and fast. I can feel the dust and stones beneath her feet. She was running to the very people she once hid from.

She had met the Messiah. She had met the Savior.

"He told me everything I've ever done!" she cried. And still—He didn't condemn her.

That's what changed her.

His gentleness helped her confront the shame she'd carried her whole life. His kindness led her to repentance.

Not fear. Not guilt. Not pressure.

Just love.

Jesus didn't focus on her sin. He focused on His promise.

Because truth be told—we don't need anyone to point out when we've messed up. We already know. We carry it. We rehearse it.

When your mind plays back your every failure…When your heart whispers every accusation—true or false…When shame follows you like a shadow…

To hear someone speak the truth—**with no condemnation… only love**—oh my…

I can feel the butterflies in her stomach.

She had just met Love.

She had met Jesus.

Seven

The Power of Forgiveness

Growing up, I was afraid. Broken. Hopeless.

I was afraid of people—afraid they could see my stains. No matter how hard I tried to hide them, I just knew… everyone knew.

And I carried so much shame. I was so broken. I didn't know how to be alive.

The best way I can describe it is this: Imagine every type of fear you can think of… and wrap it in skin and bones. That was me. One big ball of fear.

And not just fear—But shame. Hopelessness.

Like the Samaritan woman, I searched for love in all the wrong places. And like her, I found it only in Jesus—in the love and sacrifice of my Savior.

Freedom, He said. **Freedom.**

Thank You, Lord, for meeting me there this morning. Thank You for stepping into the empty places. For filling the empty holes I didn't know could ever be filled. Thank You for loving me beyond anything I've ever known—beyond anything I could have even imagined.

Thank You for taking this broken and fearful heart, this damaged soul, this weary spirit... and giving me hope. **Assured and faithful hope.**

You alone are the glory and the lifter of my head. And when the hard days come—when the enemy whispers reminders of sin and shame—thank You that perfect love casts out all fear.

"I would have lost heart...unless I had believed that I would see the goodness of the Lord in the land of the living."

Before Christ, I searched everywhere for love and acceptance. I've been up. I've been down. I've been here. I've been there.

You name it... I did it. I did it all. Too much to list here. Too much to say now.

But I remember. I remember everything. **And still... He came.**

When Jesus found me, I was shattered—beyond repair. Lost in sin and darkness. But He came.

John tells us Jesus *had* to go through Samaria. He went to meet her. **And He came to meet me.**

When Jesus found me, it was the first time in my life I wasn't afraid. For the first time, I could lift my head. For the first time...

I didn't look away. I looked into His eyes—The eyes of the One who knew me. The eyes of the One who came for me.

The Samaritan woman longed for living water. And when Jesus offered... she took it.

For the first time ever—she was alive.

Yes... She was truly alive. **And now, so am I.**

You have called *me out of darkness into Your marvelous light.*

There are no words strong enough to describe the freedom found in Jesus Christ alone.

Your love, O Lord, has brought me so far. And I know, with full confidence, that You will walk with me to the very end—until the glorious day I see You face to face.

This morning, Your love filled every wounded part of my heart. **My healing is in You, Jesus.** You are my strength. You are my song. And in all of this, Your name will be glorified.

Please, Lord… don't let my pain be wasted. Let there be purpose in my story. Use it to encourage others. To shine hope into hurting hearts. To point people to You—Jesus, the Rescuer of souls. The Healer. The Redeemer. The Savior.

My testimony is not that I stand before people clean, sober, and living right. My testimony is that I stand before Him—cleansed by His blood, forgiven, and redeemed.

Thank You, my Lord. Thank You, my Jesus.

Thank You for finding me. For saving me. For cleansing me. For healing me. For calling me Yours.

Thank You for not being ashamed of me. For loving me so much that You came and sought me out. You called me by name.

Thank You for teaching me Your ways.

> *"The law of the Lord is perfect, reviving the soul. The statutes of the Lord are trustworthy, making wise the simple. The precepts of the Lord are right, giving joy to the heart. The commands of the Lord are radiant, giving light to the eyes."*

Thank You for Your Word that breathes life into these dry bones. Thank You for Your Truth that silences the voice of the enemy. Thank You for the forgiveness of my sins.

Thank You that now—I can forgive. I can forgive those who hurt me.

But more importantly… **Thank You that I can finally forgive myself.**

Eight

Restoring What Was Lost

Jesus, thank You for the honor and joy of praying with my grandfather before he passed away—his body frail and full of cancer, but his heart open to receive You. I will see him again in Heaven.

And thank You, Lord, for my mom. A woman who loves with everything she has, everything she knows. So tender. So beautiful. So gentle. I believe—deep in my heart—that she would have done anything to protect me if she could have.

Thank You for this new life that belongs to You. My all is Yours. Do with me as You will. Teach me Your ways, O Lord. Use me for Your glory. For Your name's sake.

And Lord… thank You for covering even the parts of my past that felt unforgivable. I can't undo the abortions. I can't take back the choices I made. But You, Jesus—You met me in the deepest places of grief and shame and wrapped me in mercy. You gave me healing. You gave me hope. You gave me the promise that I will see my children again. They are safe in Your arms until the day I can hold them in mine.

Send me. Let me share You with those who are broken. Tired. Shackled by sin, shame, or failure. I know that place… Because I was there. But not anymore. No, not anymore.

Nine

Called by Name

The Samaritan woman doesn't appear again in Scripture. After her encounter with Jesus, her name is never mentioned again.

But her story—Oh, her story is told and retold again and again.

Because when Jesus calls you by name, He writes your story into eternity.

I Am Free

I used to wonder what happened to her after she left that well. But then I remember…

She was set free.

Freedom, You said. Yes, Lord…

I am finally free.

Hallelujah, I am free! AMEN.

A Letter from the One Who Redeems

From Jesus, to you.

My beloved daughter,

I see you. Not just the version of you that smiles for others, but the you behind the curtain—where the ache still lingers. I know the weight you carry, the tears you've cried in silence, the shame that tried to name you.

But you were never too far. Not for Me.

I was there in the moment it broke. I was there in the silence that followed. And I've never stopped reaching for your heart.

You are not what was done to you. You are not the lies that were spoken over you. You are not beyond healing, restoration, or joy.

You are Mine.

I traded My life so you could live in freedom—not just someday, but now. I chose the cross with your face in My mind. Not to fix you—but to *redeem* you. To restore the pieces. To breathe life into the parts that feel numb. To call you *daughter* again.

There's nothing you need to prove. No performance. No perfection. Just come. Bring Me your honest, your ugly, your undone—and I will make it beautiful in My hands.

You don't have to carry it anymore. Let Me hold you. Let Me heal you.

You were worth it. You always were.

With unshakable love,
Jesus Your Redeemer

A Letter to the Reader

Dear Reader,

Before you step into these reflection questions, I want to pause and speak directly to your heart.

This journey you've been reading isn't just about my healing—it's an invitation into your own. And at the center of that healing is a Person, not a process.

His name is Jesus. He's the One who met me in the darkest places, the One who held me when I felt unlovable, the One who whispered hope into my silence. And He's here for you too—right now, right where you are.

You don't have to have it all figured out. You don't need to clean yourself up or fix what's broken before you come to Him. He already knows every detail, every scar, every question—and He still chooses you.

Before you begin these reflections, I want to invite you to meet the One who redeems.

If you've never asked Jesus into your heart, or if you've walked away and want to come back, there's a simple prayer below to help you begin.

This isn't about religion. It's about relationship. Real. Personal. Healing.

I pray you take this step—not for me, but for you.

With love and belief in your beautiful future,
Rose

Prayer of Salvation

If you've never invited Jesus into your heart—or you're ready to come back to Him—this moment is for you.

Dear Jesus,

I believe You are the Son of God. I believe You died for my sins and rose again. I need You. I'm done trying to fix myself. I surrender my life to You—every broken piece. Come into my heart, Jesus. Be my Lord, my Savior, and my Healer. I receive Your forgiveness. I receive Your love. And I choose to follow You, all the days of my life.

In Your holy name,
Amen.

Reflection Questions

1. *In Your Search for Love and Healing:*

   Reflect on a time when, like the Samaritan woman, you sought love, worth, or healing in places that only left you feeling more broken. What were you truly longing for, and what did that reveal about your need for true acceptance in Christ?

2. *On Freedom in Christ:*

   What does "freedom in Christ" mean to you personally? Consider the areas of your life where you still feel bound or weighed down. How do you imagine Jesus setting you free?

3. *On Forgiveness and Releasing Shame:*

   Is there someone—or even a part of yourself—that you struggle to forgive? What aspects of your past still whisper shame or regret into your heart, and how can you surrender those to Christ's redeeming love?

4. *Encountering Jesus in Your Brokenness:*

   Think of a moment when Jesus met you in your deepest brokenness. How did that turning point change your perspective about your worth and healing? What does that encounter tell you about God's purpose for your pain?

5. *At the Well with Jesus:*

   Imagine Jesus sitting with you at the well right now. What do you think He would say about your search for love and healing, and how might His words invite you to embrace a deeper, transformative freedom?

Let the answers come softly. No rush. Just be still. He's not asking you to strive—He's asking you to come.

PRAYER

Heavenly Father,

Thank You for being the God who sees me, who knows me, and who still chooses me. Thank You for finding me in my brokenness and calling me by name. You are my Redeemer, my Restorer, my Safe Place.

Lord, I surrender every part of my past to You—the hurt, the shame, the regrets, and the pain. Thank You for the forgiveness You freely offer. Help me to walk in that same forgiveness toward others… and toward myself.

Teach me Your ways. Use my life for Your glory. Let my story be a beacon of hope for the hurting, a testimony of what only You can do. Thank You, Jesus, that because of You—I am free.

In Your powerful and precious name,
Amen.

SCRIPTURE FOCUS

"So if the Son sets you free, you will be free indeed." —*John 8:36*

"The Lord is close to the brokenhearted and saves those who are crushed in spirit." —*Psalm 34:18*

"He lifted me out of the slimy pit, out of the mud and mire; he set my feet on a rock and gave me a firm place to stand." —*Psalm 40:2*

"Come to me, all you who are weary and burdened, and I will give you rest." —*Matthew 11:28*

PAUSE & REFLECT

Redeemed: A Journey from Brokenness to Freedom

Take a deep breath. Let this moment settle in your spirit.

You've just read a sacred part of the journey—one that speaks of chains breaking, shame being washed away, and the Savior gently lifting your head. These next questions are meant to draw you closer to Jesus. Not to perform or prove anything. Just to be with Him. He's near.

ONE—THE SILENCE THAT SHAPED ME

Reflection Questions

1. Have you ever felt like your voice didn't matter or that your pain was ignored? What did that experience do to your heart?

2. What silent wounds or fears have you carried for too long?

3. Are there lies you've believed about your worth or identity because of what happened to you?

4. What comfort or hope do you find in knowing that God hears every silent cry and sees every hidden tear?

5. If you could speak to your younger self—the one who was hurting in silence—what would you say?

Prayer

Jesus,

You see the parts of me that no one else has ever seen. You hear the cries I've never spoken aloud. You know the fear I've carried, the shame I've buried, the silence I've lived in. Thank You for being the God who draws near—who never turns away. I give You the parts of my story that still hurt, still ache, still make me feel small. Heal what was broken in the silence.

Restore what was stolen in the shadows. Teach me how to use my voice again—not in fear, but in freedom. Thank You that my story doesn't end in silence. It ends in redemption.

Amen.

Scripture for the Soul

"You have kept count of my tossings; put my tears in your bottle. Are they not in your book?" —Psalm 56:8 (ESV)

"The Lord is close to the brokenhearted and saves those who are crushed in spirit." —Psalm 34:18 (NIV)

"He heals the brokenhearted and binds up their wounds." —Psalm 147:3 (NLT)

TWO—THE GIRL NO ONE PROTECTED

Reflection Questions

1. Have there been moments when you longed for someone to step in and protect you—but they didn't? How did that shape your view of yourself or of others?

2. What beliefs did you begin to form about your worth because of the pain others caused or allowed?

3. Can you imagine Jesus in that memory with you—what would He say to the little girl who felt unprotected?

4. What would change if you truly believed that you were never invisible to God?

5. What might it look like to begin trusting Him as your Defender now?

Prayer

Jesus,

I've carried the pain of not being protected for so long. I didn't understand why no one stood up for me. Why no one stopped what was happening. But You were there. Even when I didn't see You. Even when the silence was deafening. You never looked away. Lord, heal the places in me that still feel abandoned. Show me that I was never alone. Speak truth to the lies I believed about my worth. And when I'm tempted to carry the weight alone, remind me that You are my Defender. You call me precious. You call me whole. You call me Yours.

Amen.

Scripture for the Soul

"Even if my father and mother abandon me, the Lord will hold me close." — *Psalm 27:10 (NLT)*

"The Lord your God goes with you to fight for you… to give you victory." — *Deuteronomy 20:4 (NIV)*

"The Lord will fight for you; you need only to be still." — *Exodus 14:14 (NIV)*

THREE—TRYING TO FEEL ALIVE

Reflection Questions

1. What have you turned to in the past to escape pain or try to feel something other than empty?

2. Did any of those things actually bring healing—or did they leave you more broken?

3. What emotions or deeper wounds were you trying to numb or silence in those moments?

4. Where do you feel Jesus inviting you to let go of false comfort and let Him in today?

5. What would it look like to trust Him with that ache—and choose healing instead of numbing?

Prayer

Jesus,

You know all the ways I've tried to fill the emptiness. All the people I've run to. All the false comforts I've reached for when I didn't know what else to do. But none of it worked. None of it healed me. Today, I want to stop running from the pain and start running to You. Help me surrender the things I've clung to that only made me feel more alone. I want to feel truly alive—not in chaos, not in survival, but in You. You are the only One who satisfies. You are the only One who heals. Fill me with Your peace. Fill me with Your presence. Fill me with life that never fades.

Amen.

Scripture for the Soul

"Why spend your money on what is not bread, and your labor on what does not satisfy?" —*Isaiah 55:2 (NIV)*

"The thief comes only to steal and kill and destroy. I came that they may have life and have it abundantly." —*John 10:10 (ESV)*

"You make known to me the path of life; in Your presence there is fullness of joy." —*Psalm 16:11 (ESV)*

FOUR—I LOST MYSELF

Reflection Questions

1. Are there seasons in your life where you felt emotionally shut down, like you couldn't be fully "you"?

2. What made it feel unsafe to express or even feel your own emotions during that time?

3. What lies did you begin to believe when you were living in survival mode?

4. If that disconnected, shut-down version of you could hear one thing from Jesus today, what would you want Him to say?

5. What would it feel like to begin coming alive again—not in performance, but in His presence?

Prayer

Father,

There have been seasons where I didn't know how to keep going. Times when I lost who I was. When I felt so far away from myself—and from You. Thank You that even when I felt invisible, You saw me. Even when I shut down, You stayed close. Even when I gave up, You didn't. Lord, breathe life into the parts of me that feel numb. Help me feel again. Hope again. Live again. Bring me out of the shadows. Remind me that no matter how lost I may feel—You have never let me go.

Amen.

Scripture for the Soul

"He restores my soul. He leads me in paths of righteousness for His name's sake." —Psalm 23:3 (ESV)

"I will give you a new heart and put a new spirit in you... a heart of flesh." —Ezekiel 36:26 (NIV)

"The light shines in the darkness, and the darkness has not overcome it." —John 1:5 (NIV)

FIVE—THE WOMAN AT THE WELL

Reflection Questions

1. In what ways do you relate to the Samaritan woman—longing for love, yet carrying shame or rejection?

2. Are there "wells" in your life—relationships, behaviors, mindsets— you've turned to that still leave you empty?

3. What does it mean to your heart that Jesus sees everything you've ever done… and still loves you?

4. If Jesus was sitting beside you right now, what do you think He would say?

5. Are you ready to receive what He's offering—love that doesn't leave, water that truly satisfies?

Prayer

Jesus,

Thank You for meeting me at my well. You saw past the surface… Past my mistakes… Past my shame. And still—you stayed. You didn't look away. You offered me living water when I didn't even know I was dying of thirst. Teach me to stop running. To stop hiding. To stop trying to fill the emptiness with things that never last. Fill me with Your presence. Let Your love be the well I return to again and again. Thank You for seeing me. Thank You for loving me. Thank You for choosing me.

Amen.

Scripture for the Soul

*"Whoever drinks the water I give them will never thirst...
a spring of water welling up to eternal life."* —*John 4:14 (NIV)*

"Come, all you who are thirsty, come to the waters."
—*Isaiah 55:1 (NIV)*

"There is now no condemnation for those who are in Christ Jesus."
—*Romans 8:1 (NIV)*

SIX—WHEN HE FOUND ME

Reflection Questions

1. Can you recall a moment when you knew—deep down—that Jesus was drawing near to you?

2. What does it mean to you to be "found" by God rather than forgotten or overlooked?

3. How does your heart respond to the truth that Jesus sees your whole story and still calls you His?

4. Is there a part of your heart still hiding in fear, shame, or self-protection? What might it look like to bring that into His light?

5. If you stood face to face with Jesus, what would you want to hear Him say to you?

Prayer

Jesus,

Thank You for finding me. For coming to the dark places I thought were too far gone. You didn't ask me to clean myself up. You just came close. You called my name. You lifted my head. You looked into my eyes with love I had never known. There is no one like You. You didn't come to condemn me. You came to rescue me. So here I am, Lord. All of me. Take my story, take my scars, take my shame—and turn it all into something beautiful. I'm so grateful You found me. And I never want to be lost again.

Amen.

Scripture for the Soul

"For the Son of Man came to seek and to save the lost."
—Luke 19:10 (NIV)

"Fear not, for I have redeemed you; I have called you by name,
you are mine." —Isaiah 43:1 (ESV)

"You are a chosen people… called out of darkness into His wonderful
light." —1 Peter 2:9 (NIV)

SEVEN—THE POWER OF FORGIVENESS

Reflection Questions

1. Who have you struggled to forgive—whether it's someone else… or yourself?

2. What feelings or fears rise up when you think about letting that pain go?

3. How has unforgiveness affected your heart, your healing, or your relationships?

4. What would it look like to hand that burden to Jesus today—not in your strength, but in His grace?

5. Are you willing to begin the process of forgiveness, even if it feels slow? What might the first step be?

Prayer

Jesus,

You know the pain I've carried. You've seen the people who hurt me—the ones who left me bleeding, the ones who never said sorry. You've seen the weight I've tried to carry on my own. Today, I lay it at Your feet. Not because it didn't matter—but because it matters so much, I can't hold it anymore. Help me to forgive. Help me release them to You. Not for their sake, but for mine. So I can finally be free. And Lord…Help me to forgive myself. For the choices I made in my pain. For the shame I've worn like a label. For believing I wasn't worth anything more. Wash me in Your grace. Cover me in Your mercy. Teach me to live like someone who is truly free.

Amen.

Scripture for the Soul

"Be kind and compassionate to one another, forgiving each other, just as in Christ God forgave you." —Ephesians 4:32 (NIV)

"He does not treat us as our sins deserve or repay us according to our iniquities." —Psalm 103:10 (NIV)

"As far as the east is from the west, so far has he removed our transgressions from us." —Psalm 103:12 (NIV)

EIGHT—RESTORING WHAT WAS LOST

Reflection Questions

1. Are there parts of your life—dreams, relationships, hope—that feel too far gone to be restored?

2. Can you recognize any areas, big or small, where God has already begun rebuilding something in your story?

3. Is there something you've stopped praying about because it felt too broken? Could you bring it to Him again today?

4. How might your testimony become part of someone else's healing?

5. What would restoration look like—not just externally, but deep in your heart and identity?

Prayer

God,

You are the Restorer of all things. You don't just rescue me from the pit—You rebuild what the pit tried to destroy. Thank You for the moments of healing I've seen—the glimpses of Your hand making things new. Even when I don't understand the process, even when restoration feels slow or messy, help me trust that You are always working. I lift up to You the people and places I've given up on. The memories that still ache. The dreams I thought were dead. Breathe life into them again. Restore what was lost—according to Your will, in Your perfect time. And even if it looks different than I imagined, let it be beautiful in Your way.

Amen.

Scripture for the Soul

"I will repay you for the years the locusts have eaten."
—Joel 2:25 (NIV)

"The God of all grace… will himself restore you and make you strong."
—I Peter 5:10 (NIV)

"See, I am doing a new thing! Now it springs up; do you not perceive it?" —Isaiah 43:19 (NIV)

NINE—CALLED BY NAME

Reflection Questions

1. What false names or labels have been spoken over your life that God never gave you?

2. Have you let your past—or others' opinions—define your worth?

3. How would your life change if you fully believed you were chosen, seen, and loved by God?

4. What new name do you sense the Father whispering over you now?

5. How is He calling you to live differently in light of who He says you are?

Prayer

Father,

Thank You for calling me by name. Thank You for speaking identity over me when all I heard was lies. You never stopped pursuing me—even when I didn't know who I was. Today, I lay down every false label I've worn. Every name that came from pain, fear, or rejection. Every lie I believed about my worth. I choose to believe what You say about me: That I am loved. That I am chosen. That I am redeemed. That I am Yours. Help me live from this truth—boldly, freely, unapologetically.In You, I finally know who I am.

Amen.

Scripture for the Soul

"Do not fear, for I have redeemed you; I have summoned you by name; you are mine." —Isaiah 43:1 (NIV)

"The Spirit himself testifies with our spirit that we are God's children." —Romans 8:16 (NIV)

"To all who did receive him… he gave the right to become children of God." —John 1:12 (NIV)

_____

_____

_____

_____

_____

_____

_____

_____

_____

_____

_____

_____

_____

_____

_____

_____

_____

_____

TEN—I AM FREE

Reflection Questions

1. What does true freedom in Jesus look like for you today—not just in theory, but in practice?

2. Are there any parts of your heart still in chains—places that haven't fully stepped into that freedom?

3. How has God's grace already rewritten parts of your story—and where is He still writing?

4. Who might need to hear your story of healing, hope, and redemption?

5. What would it mean to walk boldly, unashamed, and fully free as a redeemed daughter of the King?

Prayer

Jesus,

Thank You for setting me free. For breaking every chain that held me back. For silencing the shame that tried to define me. For rewriting my story with mercy and love. I stand here not as someone who has it all together—but as someone held together by Your grace. Thank You that my past no longer has power over me. That fear no longer owns me. That I can lift my head—because You have lifted me. Let my life shout freedom to those still in the dark. Let my story lead others to the well. To You. To healing. To freedom.

Amen.

Scripture for the Soul

"So if the Son sets you free, you will be free indeed."
—John 8:36 (NIV)

"Now the Lord is the Spirit, and where the Spirit of the Lord is, there is freedom." —2 Corinthians 3:17 (NIV)

"It is for freedom that Christ has set us free." —Galatians 5:1 (NIV)

_____

_____

_____

_____

_____

_____

_____

_____

_____

_____

_____

_____

_____

_____

_____

_____

_____

_____

One Last Thing

If you're reading this and you feel changed—thank God. If you're reading this and you still feel unsure—thank God, too.

Because He finishes what He starts.

This isn't the end of your healing. It's the beginning of deeper freedom, deeper intimacy, and deeper peace. Keep walking. Keep pressing in. Jesus isn't finished with you yet—and what He started, He will complete.

You are seen. You are held. You are so deeply loved. Keep going.

—Rose

BONUS

Unfiltered—A Journal from the Pain

Written in the thick of it—before healing, before hope, before I knew Jesus.

(*This is a page from my journal, written long before I knew Jesus. It's not polished. It's not edited. It's exactly how I felt in the middle of my pain. I share it not for shock, but for honesty. Because someone, somewhere, may still be in this place. And I want her to know—this is not where her story has to end*)

The abuse started so early. I was so young. My heart both cringes and cries when I think of the grooming and all the manipulation over the years. I was so young. It's shameful... I can barely say the words. It's heavy. I feel the weight of the memories still. And it's ugly. It's terrifying.

Like a monster that continually surrounds you until you are covered and dripping in fear...Then shame devours you. The only way I can describe it, is to call it what it is. It's a mindf*%&.

That's what it is. You can't make sense of all of it, let alone move beyond it.

The thoughts are constant. And it's just all so much to carry around.

The shame. The fear. The sadness. It's so heavy...

Mindf*&%. It wins, end of story. No matter what you say or what you try or even what you do, it wins. You're f*&%. You will never be able to reconcile it. Ever.

Edit: But wait.

I wrote this and at the time did not believe there was any hope for freedom.

But I was wrong.

There is hope.

His name is Jesus.

AFTERTHOUGHT—"OVERFLOW"

If I could stand on the rooftop with my hands lifted high and tears running down my face, I would scream this with everything in me:

JESUS HAS REDEEMED ME!!

He didn't just save me—He *freed* me. He didn't just patch me up—He made me *new*. He didn't just whisper "I love you"—He *proved it* with every drop of blood, every ounce of mercy, every miracle along the way. I am absolutely overflowing. With joy. With wonder. With the kind of love that makes your chest ache in the best way possible.

I can't stop smiling. I can't stop crying. I can't stop praising. Because *look what the Lord has done!*

This joy? It's not surface level. It's soul deep. It's the kind that wakes you up singing and lays you down grateful. It's laughter in the middle of scars. It's dancing with the lights on and the windows open. It's knowing—I AM REDEEMED.

And now, sweet friend…This story isn't just mine anymore. It's yours too.

Thank you for reading these pages. Thank you for stepping into the sacred. But even more—thank you for daring to believe that this kind of freedom is for *you*, too.

Because it is. Oh my goodness, it *so is*.

I don't know your whole story—but I know the ache of silent tears. The weight of shame. The question that whispers, *"Can God really heal someone like me?"*

And I need you to hear me say this:

YES. HE. CAN. And He *will.*

Jesus came for the ones like us. The ones who've cried behind closed doors, who've been called too broken, too loud, too complicated. The ones who thought they had to hide their hurt to belong.

But here's the truth: You belong to Him. You are His beloved. And He is rewriting your story with joy ink and resurrection power.

If all you walk away with is this—you are NOT too far gone—then every word was worth it.

If you find yourself smiling again… If hope starts rising in your chest… If you begin to believe there's more—*so much more*—then I'm celebrating with you right now.

This isn't the end. It's the beginning of something holy. Something joy-soaked and heaven-kissed.

So keep going, beautiful one. Keep healing. Keep laughing. Keep praising. Keep letting Jesus love you back to life.

And when you forget who you are? Run back to the well. He'll remind you.

You are seen. You are chosen. You are wildly loved. You are REDEEMED. You are FREE.

Dancing with joy beside you, Rose

"The Lord has done great things for us, and we are filled with joy."
—*Psalm 126:3 (NIV)*

"I pray that God, the source of hope, will fill you completely with joy and peace because you trust in Him. Then you will overflow with confident hope through the power of the Holy Spirit."
—*Romans 15:13 (NLT)*

"I delight greatly in the Lord; my soul rejoices in my God. For He has clothed me with garments of salvation and arrayed me in a robe of His righteousness..." —Isaiah 61:10 (NIV)

"You turned my wailing into dancing; you removed my sackcloth and clothed me with joy, that my heart may sing your praises and not be silent. Lord my God, I will praise you forever." —Psalm 30:11-12 (NIV)

·

WHY I CHOSE TO WRITE THIS WAY
A note from my heart...

If you're still here, reading these words—I just want to pause and say thank you.

Thank you for walking through the pages of my story with such tenderness.

Thank you for letting me be real. For letting me point to Jesus.

Before you close this book, there's one last thing I need to share with you—something I carried quietly the whole time I was writing. A piece of my heart behind every word...

Some people may have picked up *Redeemed* expecting to read every gritty detail of what I went through—the abuse, the trauma, the heartbreak. Others may have been curious about the sins I fell into—the decisions I made, the struggles I faced, the mess I created.

And I get that. When someone says they've been through something, we naturally want to know. We want the story, the facts, the receipts. But from the very beginning, I knew this book wasn't going to be about the gory details.

Yes, the pain was real. The trauma ran deep. There were moments so dark I didn't think I'd survive them—seasons where I felt invisible, shattered, and completely undone. I could've written chapters that would've broken your heart and left you in tears, that would make you angry on my behalf, that would draw sympathy or even horror and shock. But I didn't.

Not because I'm hiding anything, but because I'm protecting something.

My healing.

You see, Jesus didn't meet me at the edge of my trauma so I could relive it on paper—He met me there to redeem it. And that's the story I wanted to tell. Not the horror, but the healing. Not the shame, but the Savior.

This book isn't about pointing fingers or calling out names. It's not about exposing people. It's about exalting Jesus.

And when it comes to the sinful parts of my past—the rebellion, the coping, the mess I made trying to survive—I chose not to dwell there either. Not because I'm afraid to admit where I've been, but because I never wanted to glorify the sin. That's not the story I was called to tell.

I wanted to glorify the Savior.

Yes, I've sinned. Yes, I've failed. Yes, I've made choices that broke God's heart and my own. But He met me there too. And instead of rehashing every poor decision I made, I chose to focus on the grace that covered it, the truth that set me free, and the Word that renewed my mind.

The miracle isn't in the mess—it's in what God did with it.

So if you came here hoping for the shocking details, you didn't find them.

But if you came here looking for hope, for healing, for something real that points you back to the heart of God—then I pray you found exactly what you needed.

Because my story isn't about how bad it was.

It's about how good He is.

Will there ever be a time I go into deeper detail? Maybe.

Perhaps there will come a day—when the Holy Spirit leads—where I share more of the hard stuff, the moments I've only ever whispered to Jesus.

But *Redeemed* wasn't that book.

This was a one-morning journaling session that turned into a testimony.

A sacred, unexpected moment where God told me to write—not to revisit every wound, but to release what He had healed.

So I followed His lead.

And I trust that if He ever calls me to go deeper, He'll meet me there too.

With grace and gratitude, and a heart that prays you feel His love on every page,

Rose

"Come and see what God has done, His awesome deeds for mankind!"
—Psalm 66:5 (NIV)

Prayer

Jesus, thank You for meeting me in the wreckage and calling me by my name. Thank You for healing what no one else could, and for using every broken piece to point back to You. I pray for the woman reading this right now—the one who's carrying her own pain, who wonders if she has to tell it all in order to be heard. Remind her that her story is safe with You. Remind her that she doesn't have to glorify the sin to glorify the Savior. Use her life, Lord, as a living testimony of Your mercy, Your power, and Your never-ending love. In Your holy name, amen.

Stay Connected

Want more encouragement, updates, and resources on your healing journey?

Visit **rosemetheny.com**

- *Blog posts, book updates, and more from Rose*
- Join the email list for devotionals, freebies, and behind-the-scenes.
- Explore the full *Redeemed* and *Renewed* collection. Let's keep walking in freedom—together.

You can also reach out directly at:
hello@rosemetheny.com